DINOSAURS

A Matter-of-Fact Book

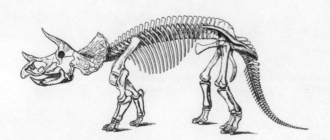

Written by
MARTIN L. KEEN

Illustrated by
JOHN HULL
MATTHEW KALMENOFF
R.F. PETERSEN

Design, Layout, and Editorial Production by
DONALD D. WOLF and MARGOT L. WOLF

Grosset & Dunlap • Publishers • New York

Some of the material in this book originally appeared in
The Wonders of Prehistoric Life, published by Grosset & Dunlap, Inc.

Library of Congress Catalog Number: 82-80881
ISBN: 0-448-04084-0

Contents

CENOZOIC ERA 60 MILLION YEARS	**CENOZOIC PERIOD**	PLIOCENE EPOCH	A G E O F M A M M A L S
		MIOCENE EPOCH	
		OLIGOCENE EPOCH	
		EOCENE EPOCH	
		PALEOCENE EPOCH	
		1-60 MILLION YEARS AGO	

MASTODON
EOHIPPUS
MEGATHERIUM

MESOZOIC ERA 120 MILLION YEARS	**CRETACEOUS PERIOD** 130 MILLION YEARS AGO	AGE OF REPTILES
	JURASSIC PERIOD 155 MILLION YEARS AGO	
	TRIASSIC PERIOD 185 MILLION YEARS AGO	AGE OF REPTILES

MIXOSAURUS
TYRANNOSAURUS

PALEOZOIC ERA 335 MILLION YEARS	**PERMIAN PERIOD** 210 MILLION YEARS AGO	AGE OF REPTILES
	CARBONIFEROUS PERIOD 265 MILLION YEARS AGO	COAL AGE
	DEVONIAN PERIOD 320 MILLION YEARS AGO	AGE OF FISH
	SILURIAN PERIOD 360 MILLION YEARS AGO	AGE OF INVERTEBRATES
	ORDOVICIAN PERIOD 440 MILLION YEARS AGO	
	CAMBRIAN PERIOD 520 MILLION YEARS AGO	

DIMETRODON
EUSTHENOPTERON
SALTOPOSUCHUS

PLACODERM
EURYPTERID
LAMP SHELL
CORAL

PRE-CAMBRIAN ERA	600 MILLION YEARS AGO	AGE OF HIDDEN LIFE
	4-5 BILLION YEARS AGO	NO LIVING THINGS
	4½ BILLION YEARS AGO	DEEP PART OF EARTH'S CRUST FORMED
	5 BILLION YEARS AGO	APPROXIMATE BEGINNING OF EARTH AS PLANET

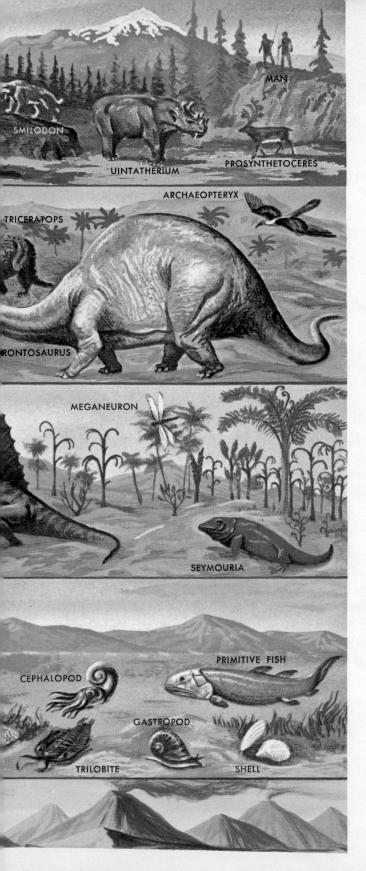

SMILODON

UINTATHERIUM

MAN

PROSYNTHETOCERES

ARCHAEOPTERYX

TRICERATOPS

RONTOSAURUS

MEGANEURON

SEYMOURIA

CEPHALOPOD

PRIMITIVE FISH

GASTROPOD

TRILOBITE

SHELL

The Record of Past Life

When Vice President-elect Thomas Jefferson arrived in the nation's capital, Philadelphia, in 1797, he brought with him a special box from his home. The box contained many large bones and claws that had been found on the floor of a cave in western Virginia. Two years later, Jefferson delivered an address to the American Philosophical Society, describing the animal from which he believed the bones and claws had come. He called the animal *Megalonyx*, or "great claw." He believed the Megalonyx to be a gigantic lion, and he thought that some of these lions might yet be roaming the great forests of the American West and Northwest.

Today we know that the bones Jefferson studied really belonged to a huge ground sloth that lived millions of years ago in what is now North America. Scientists call this sloth *Megalonyx jeffersoni* in honor of the discoverer of its bones. The Megalonyx was a huge, hairy animal that walked on the sides of its four long-clawed feet, as today's sloths do. It had a thick, hairy tail upon which it could rest some of its weight. The Megalonyx, only one of hundreds of creatures that lived in the past, is a *prehistoric* animal.

You know that the word history means "a record of past events." Since "pre-" means "before," you can see that prehistoric means "before a record of past events." More accurately, prehistoric means "before a *written* record of past events," because, as we shall learn, many events that took place in long-past ages have left clear and abundant records in the earth itself.

The chart shows the history of life on earth as revealed in the record of the rocks. It shows the eras and periods that are explained on pages 6 and 7 of this book, and it shows the form of life dominant in each phase of the earth's geological history. You can see how late the mammals appeared and how "recently" human beings emerged.

Every bit of evidence we have of prehistoric life has been found in the rocks that make up the top of the earth's crust. So, before we can learn about prehistoric life, we must know some things about these rocks.

The earth is probably five billion years old. In this great span of time, the earth has undergone many changes. Scientists believe that during the first half billion years the earth consisted of molten rock. Some time between 4 and 4½ billion years ago, the molten rock cooled enough to form a solid, smooth crust around the earth. Beneath the crust, the rock remained very hot and soft.

In the last four billion years the crust changed greatly. The smooth, rocky surface folded and cracked in many places. Vast blocks of lighter rock, floating on the molten rock beneath the crust, formed the earth's continents. Heavier blocks sank, making depressions into which water poured to form the seas that cover three-quarters of the earth's surface.

Time after time, very slow movements of the huge blocks of the crust caused mountain chains to form where the blocks collided. Other mountains were formed from the lava and ashes spewed forth by volcanoes. And time after time, rain and the running water of streams and rivers wore the mountains down to sea level.

As the earth changed, the seas overran the continents many times. Large areas of North America were covered by great shallow seas and vast swamps. Today, farmers plowing in Kansas sometimes turn up shells from beds of clams that lived 100 million years ago in the sea that covered much of the Middle West.

About a billion years ago, the first living things appeared on earth. We do not know what they were, but it is believed that each consisted of only a single cell of living matter. The first living things of which we have any record are *algae*, single-celled plants that lived in colonies, much as do the algae of today. (You know algae as seaweed, or as the green or brown slimy growth that you may have seen on the surface of a pond. You may also find algae as the emerald-green covering on the shady side of trees and rocks.) The earliest animals of which we know are sponges. Also living in the very early period of life on earth were corals and probably jellyfish. All these things lived in the warm seas that covered much of the earth's surface.

In order to locate events in the very long history of the earth, scientists have divided past time into several units. As you learn about these units, it will help you to understand them if you refer to the chart on pages 4-5. On the left hand side of the chart you will see four main divisions called *eras*. As mentioned earlier, there have been times in the past when movements of the earth's crust have formed great mountain chains. At the same time, there was an increase in the number of active volcanoes, which also resulted in mountain building. These periods of rapid mountain building are called *revolutions*. The great spans of time between revolutions are eras. Since eras are the longest divisions of earth-time, they could be called the volumes in the book of the earth's history.

During each era, smaller movements of the earth's crust formed mountains and highlands; running water wore the high places down, and the oceans invaded the continents, forming shallow seas; then the land began to rise again, and the shallow inland seas receded and disappeared. This series of events took place time after time, and each of these series is called a *period*. We can think of periods as chapters in the volumes of the earth's history.

Each one of the stages within a period—the folding of the crust and the advance and retreat of the seas—marks an *epoch* in the earth's history. Epochs are the pages in the chapters of the earth's history.

There is still another unit of earth time. This unit is the *age*, and it refers to the kind of living things that dominated a time span. The Age of Hidden Life, the Age of Fishes, the Age of Reptiles, and the Age of Mammals are some of the different ages of earth time.

As we learn more about the history of life on earth, we shall be talking about millions, hundreds of millions, and billions of years. Let us try to form an idea of what these large numbers mean. Suppose that a ten-year-old boy were to begin to count at the rate of two every second. And suppose that this boy were to continue to count for eight hours a day, five days a week, and fifty weeks a year. If this boy began to count on a Monday, he would not reach one million until Wednesday morning of the fourth week of his counting. He would have to count for more than 7½ months to reach 10 million. He would be nearly seventeen years old by the time he had counted to 100 million. Before he reached a billion, he would be long past the time when most persons retire from work. He would not count the words "one billion" until the first month of his seventy-seventh year.

When you read about great numbers of years, remember how long it takes someone to count that number at the rate of two every second.

There are two ways in which prehistoric events have left a record. The record of what has happened to the crust of the earth is revealed to us in rocks. The record of past life is revealed by fossils, which are the remains of living things of the distant past.

Prehistoric North American tar pits, like the La Brea Tar Pits of California, were filled with a sticky mixture of soil and petroleum. These pits were often death traps for animals.

THE RECORD FROM THE FOSSILS

A fossil is preserved evidence of prehistoric plant or animal life. Fossils begin to form when the hard parts of dead animals, such as bones, teeth, claws, and shells are buried in river mud, desert sand, or ashes from volcanoes. Burial protects the animal parts from decay. In millions of years, the mud, sand, or ashes turns into rock. So do the animal parts within the rock. Whole skeletons of animals have been preserved in this way. So when we read about dinosaur bones, we usually mean fossil bones—the rocky forms of the bones, not the real bones.

Sometimes whole plants or animals became fossils by being trapped in some substance that preserved them from decay. Amber is one such substance. Amber looks like clear, dark yellow plastic. Amber is itself a fossil of the sticky yellow pitch that oozes from the bark of pine trees.

Fossils of insects have been found encased in amber, originally a sticky resin oozing from tree trunks.

Ice is another substance that has preserved animal remains. At the left is a picture of a cast made in Russia from a frozen woolly mammoth. The animal was buried for 20,000 years.

Volcanic ashes are another preserver of past life. Below is the "dog of Pompeii," trapped when Mount Vesuvius erupted in A.D. 79.

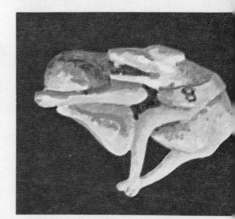

Fossils of insects, leaves, and twigs have been found encased in amber. These living things became caught in the sticky pitch on the trunks and limbs of trees and, after a time, were covered completely by the oozing pitch. Long contact with the air hardened the pitch. The trees died, fell, and decayed. The hardened pitch was buried in the earth and eventually became fossil amber.

Tar and asphalt are other substances that can preserve animal remains from decay. Thousands of skeletons of animals have been found in tar and asphalt pits. These pits may at one time have been covered by water. Animals drinking this water became stuck in the tar and were unable to pull themselves free. These trapped animals sank beneath the surface of the tar. The tar hardened into asphalt and preserved the animals buried in it. The Rancho La Brea Tar Pits, near Los Angeles, California, are famous for the thousands of beautifully preserved skeletons that have been dug out of them. Horses, mammoths, wolves, large saber-toothed cats, and vultures are among the animals that were trapped in these tar pits.

Ice is a third substance that has preserved animal remains. In Alaska and Siberia whole carcasses of mammoths and rhinoceroses have been found in frozen mud. These animals were found entirely as they were when alive. Bones, skin, hair, toenails, internal organs, and even food in the stomachs of these fossil animals were preserved. Frozen fossils are only about

This fossil is a plant impression encased in rock.

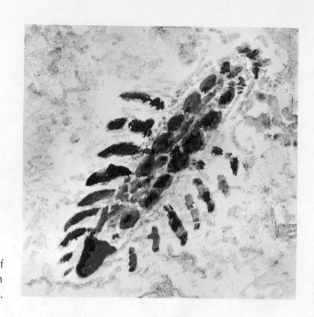

At right are the fossil remains of a Xenusion embedded in Precambrian sandstone.

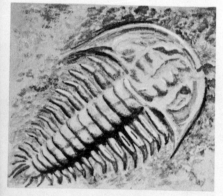

Fossilized Trilobite embedded in rock.

20,000 years old—not very old when compared with the millions of years by which the age of most fossils is measured.

By far the most common fossils are those that are *petrified*, or turned to stone. When sand or sediment slowly turns into rock, water seeping among the grains dissolves the bones of the buried animal completely; but minerals dissolved in the water slowly replace the original material of the body. The result is a stone cast, or model, of the skeleton.

Plants become petrified, too. The most famous petrified plant fossils are those found in the Petrified Forest of Arizona. The trees of this forest were buried and became petrified. Millions of years later, wind and water uncovered the forest.

Sometimes fossils were formed when ashes from volcanoes covered dead plants and animals. The ashes kept the once-living things from decaying. There are valleys in Oregon and Colorado where such fossils have been found. Poisonous gases from a volcano killed nearby plants and animals. Ashes from the volcano buried the dead. The ashes turned to a kind of rock called tuff, and within the tuff the dead plants and animals became petrified. In Yellowstone National Park there is a cliff that contains seventeen petrified forests, one on top of the other. All the forests are buried in ashes from volcanoes.

The study of prehistoric life through fossils is *paleontology* (pale-ee-ahn-TAHL-uh-gee), a word that means "to speak of ancient beings" or "to study ancient life." The women and men who work at paleontology are called *paleontologists*.

THE RECORD OF THE ROCKS

There are three kinds of rocks. Those that hardened from molten material, which sometimes rise to the earth's surface from beneath the earth's crust, are called *igneous* (IG-nee-us), or "fire-made," rocks. Quartz is an igneous rock; so are granite and basalt.

All kinds of rocks that are on the surface of the earth are eventually worn down and broken into small grains by the action of weather and running water. Streams and rivers carry the rock grains to the lowlands and to the seas. Rock grains that are carried by running water are called *sediment*. Sediment piles up on the lowlands when rivers flood, and it piles up in the sea at the mouths of rivers. Millions of tons of sediment pile up until they cause the solid rock beneath it to bend downward. In some places sediment has piled more than ten miles thick. To reach such great thicknesses, the piling-up process had to continue for scores of millions of years.

When grains of sediment are piled to such great thicknesses, the upper layers exert tremendous pressure on the lower layers. This great pressure first squeezes the water from between the grains; then it cements the grains together into solid rock. Rocks formed in this matter are called *sedimentary* (sed-ih-MEN-tary) rocks. Sandstone is a sedimentary rock formed from compressed and cemented sand grains.

Rock grains are not the only source of sedimentary rock. Vast areas of the earth are covered for great depths by a kind of rock called limestone. The sediment that forms limestone comes from the breaking and grinding up of coral and the shells of dead shellfish. The grains of this sediment are made of

Sandstone is a typical sedimentary rock.

Metamorphic rocks are formed when heat and pressure change igneous and sedimentary rocks. Marble is changed limestone.

Igneous rocks, such as granite, form underground when molten rock matter cools.

11

PROCAMELUS

UINTATHERIUM

HOPLOPHONEUS

SYNDYOCERAS

The animals above may look strange and unfamiliar to you, but they are not creations of fiction. They all once lived in prehistoric times. Some died out, and others developed into animals living today. All of them are mammals that roamed the earth after the Age of Reptiles had ended. The changes in climate and living conditions favored the survival of the mammals over the earlier vertebrates.

While the animals above once really lived, the creatures on the opposite page are man-made. Some were created by ancient people as gods, some were just made up for fun by storytellers to entertain or to frighten their listeners. They never existed, but all of them have parts of known animals.

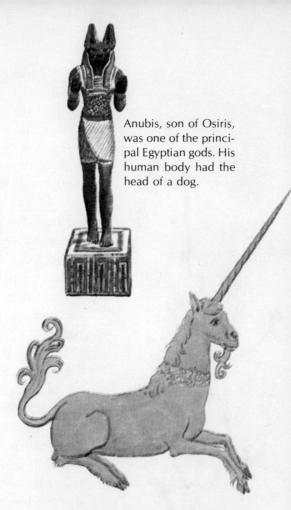

Anubis, son of Osiris, was one of the principal Egyptian gods. His human body had the head of a dog.

BARYLAMBDA

The Unicorn, said to elude every hunter, had a single long horn.

The Sphinx, a creature from many mythologies, had the head of a human on the body of a lion.

The Centaur from Greek legend had the head, trunk, and arms of a man on the body of a horse.

13

MIDDLE DEVONIAN FERNS

a chalklike material, sometimes called lime. Throughout the hundreds of millions of years since coral animals and shellfish first existed, their ground-up shells have accumulated in vast deposits on the floors of shallow seas. Time and again, the shallow seas have dried up, and the slow, powerful wrinkling movements of the earth's crust have squeezed the chalky deposits with immense pressure. As a result, the grains of these deposits have been compressed to solid rock. This kind of sedimentary rock is called limestone.

Deep beneath the earth's crust, the rock is very hot and is of a waxy softness. Rock in this condition is called *magma*. In various places, masses of magma slowly push upward into the rocks of the crust. These rocks are subjected to great heat and pressure, and as a result they are changed to rocks of a different kind. For example, when a deposit of limestone is invaded by a mass of magma, the limestone is changed to marble. Rocks formed in this manner are called *metamorphic* (met-uh-MOR-fik), or "changed-form," rocks.

Persons who know how rocks and fossils are formed can learn much about the past history of the earth by studying rocks in many parts of the world. Suppose you find a layer of basalt, an igneous rock. On the basalt is a layer of siltstone, a sedimentary rock formed from compressed mud. And on top of the siltstone is a layer of limestone. The layer of basalt tells you that at one time molten rock flowed over this area. The siltstone tells you that after the molten rock had cooled, it was covered by a lake or river. The limestone tells you that still later a shallow sea covered the same area. Also, you know that the lowest layer had to be formed first and the layers above formed later, with the uppermost layer last. (Rare exceptions to this rule are found where the folding action of the earth's crust has turned layers of rock completely upside down.)

Sedimentary rocks can also tell you approximately how long it took for them to be formed. Geologists—scientists who study the earth—have learned how long it takes for a certain thickness of each kind of sedimentary rock to form. For example, it may take 20,000 years to form one foot of a certain kind of rock. Then, if you find a cliff 500 feet high made of this rock, you know it took 10 million years to form.

Rocks reveal a continuous record of life. During the approximately 600 million years since the first living things left their fossil record in the rocks, one kind of plant and animal has succeeded another in an unbroken line of living things. The earth's crust has undergone great changes that have been accompanied by drastic changes in climate and other living conditions. There have been hot dry epochs, mild wet epochs, and epochs when ice sheets covered much of the earth. These changes have brought to an end the existence of thousands of kinds of plants and animals, but at no time was all life destroyed.

All these things may be learned by studying the record set forth in the rocks.

The Succession of Living Things

THE AGE OF HIDDEN LIFE

We have learned that the first living things of which we have records were algae, sponges, and possibly some kind of worm. In the warm seas of very early times, however, there probably were many other kinds of living things of which we have no fossil record. Because of the lack of fossils, this period of the earth's history has been named the *Cryptozoic* eon (KRIP-to-zo-ik EE-on). Cryptozoic means "hidden animal life," and an eon is a long time of no exact length. This same period of time is also called the *Precambrian* (pree-KAM-bree-un) period, for a reason we shall soon learn.

CAMBRIAN JELLYFISH

One reason for believing that there were many kinds of living things in the Cryptozoic eon is that in the rocks in the layer just above those formed in this eon we find a large variety of fossils. The animals that formed these fossils must have been living for millions of years, because they had legs, eyes, mouths, nerves, and muscles. The time in which these fossil bearing rocks were formed is called the *Cambrian* (KAM-bree-un) period. It began about 520 million years ago and lasted 80 million years.

In the warm seas that covered much of the earth during the Cambrian period there was a great number of different kinds of living things. Chief among them were *trilobites* (TRY-lo-bites), animals that were so named because their bodies were formed in three lobes; that is, they were trilobed. They had more than twenty legs on each side, and their bodies were covered with a horny material like that which covers crabs today. The smallest trilobites were less than half an inch long, the longest were twenty-eight inches, but the average was about one-and-a-half inches. They were carnivorous, which means that they ate other animals.

LIFE ON LAND BEGINS

The next period was the *Ordovician* (or-doe-VISH-un), which was also 80 million years long. Dominating life in the Ordovician seas were the *nautilids* (NAW-til-ids), animals with long, tapering shells. From the large end of the shell, a head with two eyes protruded. Growing out of the head were as many as ten tentacles, in much the same manner as those of the cuttlefish of today. Nautilids varied in length from six inches to giants of fifteen feet. They ate trilobites.

By the end of the Ordovician period, the first living things appeared on land. They were mosses, much like those we see today.

The 40 million-year period that began 360 million years ago was the *Silurian* (si-LOO-ree-un) period. All animal life still lived in the sea. King crabs appeared during this time, and they have changed only a little in appearance in all the hundreds of millions of years from the Silurian period to the present. The first fishes appeared, too. There were many kinds, but none of them were more than three or four inches long. The form of life that dominated this period was the sea scorpion. These animals looked very much like the scorpions that live on land today. There were many kinds of sea scorpions, varying in length from two-inch pygmies to nine-foot giants.

At the end of the Silurian period, mosses developed into new kinds of plants. Among them were the first ferns.

THE PERIOD OF GREATEST CHANGE

The period that began 320 million years ago and lasted 55 million years is the *Devonian* (dee-VO-nee-un) period. It brought about a dramatic change in the land areas of the world. The mosses and ferns developed into many different kinds and covered the naked rocks of the land with a green carpet. As the new plants died by the millions, their decaying remains mixed with grains of sediment left by the retreating seas, and the first soil was formed.

In this soil, ever more abundant plants grew. The soil was able to hold moisture as well as minerals needed by plants. As plants helped to form soil, they were able gradually to grow farther and farther away from shore. All the many different kinds of plants reproduced by means of spores—just as today's ferns do. The spores were carried by wind and water, and plants sprang up in new locations. In Devonian time, the climate was usually mild and wet all over the world.

In the seas, many kinds of large fish appeared and dominated the seas, and the Devonian period is also called the Age of Fishes.

In this period, the first animal to live on land came out of the seas. Some scientists think it was a sea scorpion; others think it was a lungfish, because a lungfish has gills that enable it to live under water as a fish does, and also lungs that enable it to breathe air as a land animal does. Still other scientists believe that the first land animal was one of the centipedelike creatures that lived in the sea.

Whichever may have been first, descendants of all three kinds of animals were living on land by the end of the Devonian period. The lungfish developed strong fins with which it could push itself about on mud flats during dry seasons. In later lungfish generations, these strong fins developed into the legs of the lungfish's descendant, the first *amphibian* (am-FIB-ee-un). From sea scorpions and sea centipedes came land-living scorpions and centipedes, and from these came spiders and, finally, true insects.

From nearly bare land to green forests, from fins and gills in the sea to lungs and legs on land—these were the changes wrought by the slow passage of the 55 million years of the Devonian period. There were greater changes during this period than in any other time of equal length in the history of the earth.

THE AGE OF AMPHIBIANS

In the next 55 million years, the coal deposits of North America were formed. Coal is composed almost entirely of the chemical element *carbon*, and for this reason these coal-forming years are called the *Carboniferous* (kar-bon-IF-er-us) period, or the Coal Age. During most of this period, shallow seas flooded North America, and much of the land was swampy. The climate was hot and rainy. The plants that spread over the land during the Devonian period now became thick forests of tall trees. These trees were not woody, nor did they have bark as today's trees do. Instead, they were soft and spongy, and their trunks were green.

In the steamy swamps, the trees grew rapidly, forming thick forests. The trees grew so close together that the sun could not break through their ranks to shine on the mud and water beneath. When these trees died, they fell into the water of the swamps. The fallen trees sank into the mud. More trees died and fell upon those already buried. More mud covered the newly fallen trees. The weight of the fallen trees and the mud pressed heavily on the trees that were buried deeply. Later, tremendous pressure caused by the earth's moving crust squeezed the remains of the buried trees. In somewhat the same way that pressure changed sediment into rock, the buried trees were changed into coal.

In the hot, swampy forests of the Coal Age, many scorpions and spiders crawled among the trees. Dragonflies with wingspreads of thirty inches preyed on four-inch cockroaches.

The most important animals of the Coal Age were descendants of the

While the giant amphibians still were kings of the land, other creatures evolved that scientists later called reptiles, which means "those who creep." At right, Protoceratops hatching.

lungfish, the amphibians. There are amphibians living today; among them are frogs, newts, salamanders, and toads. Amphibians live close to water, because, although they have lungs that breathe air and legs on which they can move about on land, amphibians must lay their eggs in water. The newly hatched amphibians have no legs and have gills, so they must live in water. As the young amphibians grow, they lose their gills and develop air-breathing lungs and legs. You probably are familiar with these facts, because you know that frogs hatch from eggs, becoming tadpoles that live under water.

By the end of the Coal Age, there were many kinds of amphibians running and swimming in the coal swamps. One of these was *Eryops* (ER-ee-ops), which looked like a huge tadpole with a wide flat head and body, short legs, and a flattened tail. It was as big as an alligator.

THE AGE OF REPTILES

Following the Coal Age came the *Permian* (PER-mee-un) period, which was cool and dry. It lasted 25 million years and was the beginning of the Age of Reptiles, which was about 150 million years long.

Seed plants appeared in the Permian period. One kind, called a

18

cordaite, had a smooth trunk, long straplike leaves, and big clusters of seeds among the leaves. Another kind of tree was an evergreen, or *conifer*, like a modern spruce, fir, pine, or cypress tree.

By the time the Permian period came to a close, the last trilobites had died in the sea, after a history of more than 300 million years.

At the end of the Permian period, a great amount of folding of the earth's crust took place. Many new ranges of mountains were formed, and much of the land areas of the world were high above the sea. As we have learned, a great amount of mountain-building signals the end of an era, one of the volumes in the book of the earth's history. The era whose periods we have just read about is called the *Paleozoic* (PALE-ee-uh-ZO-ik) era, or era of ancient life.

Because reptiles did not have to lay their eggs in water, they had an advantage over amphibians. Reptiles did not have to remain near water, but could range far inland in search of food. As a result, reptiles increased greatly in kinds and numbers. By the end of the Permian period, reptiles were well on their way to becoming the dominant form of life on land.

The next volume in the book of prehistoric history is the *Mesozoic* (MES-uh-ZO-ik) era, or era of middle life. The Mesozoic era lasted 120 million years and had three periods. These were the *Triassic* (try-ASS-ik), *Jurassic* (joo-RASS-ik), and *Cretaceous* (kree-Tay-shuss). When compared to the Paleozoic, the climate of the Mesozoic was dry. Although each period had the flooding, most of the floods were smaller than those of periods in the Paleozoic era.

During the Triassic period, bony fish became the main kind of fish. All the many other kinds that had existed before this time died out—except for sharks and a few others, such as lamprey eels.

By far the most abundant and most dominant form of life in the Mesozoic era were reptiles. Indeed, the Mesozoic is also called the Age of Reptiles. Great numbers of reptiles of many kinds lived in this era. They invaded all parts of the land, sea, and even the air. There are many reptiles living today. Among them are alligators, crocodiles, snakes, lizards, and tortoises.

Fossils do not tell us what colors the prehistoric reptiles were, but since many modern reptiles are clothed in bright colors of beautiful design, the ancient reptiles also were probably colored brightly.

The "grandfather" of all reptiles was *Seymouria* (see-Moor-ee-ya), named for the town of Seymour, Texas, near where its fossil was first found. The body of Seymouria was held close to the ground on short legs that extended out from the sides, as the legs of amphibians do. But Seymouria

While Edaphosaurus was a plant-eater, his "cousin" Dimetrodon was a meat-eater, who, as often as he could catch him, put his "cousin" in his diet.

EDAPHOSAURUS

laid its eggs on land, as reptiles do. So, you can see that it was a link between amphibians and reptiles.

Among the earliest of the true reptiles was *Dimetrodon* (dye-MET-ruh-don), a name meaning "double-measure tooth," because it had teeth of two sizes. Both sizes were sharp, for grasping and eating the fish that were Dimetrodon's food. It had a long body and tail and short legs, so it rested close to the ground. Along the top of its back it had a tail fin-like "sail." Some scientists think the sail had many blood vessels, and thus was an organ that helped to cool Dimetrodon. Blood from its body, flowing through the blood vessels in the sail, would lose heat to the air. Then, the cooled blood would

DIMETRODONS

flow down into Dimetrodon's body, cooling it. Or, if Dimetrodon were cold, the sun shining on the sail would warm this reptile.

Another reptile that lived at the beginning of the Mesozoic was *Phytosaur* (fite-uh-SAWR), which means "plant lizard." It was given this name because scientists first thought it was a plant eater. Later, they understood that phytosaurs were giant crocodiles, and definitely were *carnivores*, or meat eaters. They looked like crocodiles that are living today, except that their nostrils were near their eyes instead of at the end of their snouts. After millions of years, phytosaurs died out, so they were not the ancestors of today's crocodiles and alligators.

DINOSAURS

The most interesting reptiles were the dinosaurs (dye-nuh-SAWRS), whose name means "terrible lizards." Among them were the largest land animals that ever lived. The largest animal that has ever lived is alive today. It is the blue whale which may grow to a length of 100 feet (30 meters) and weigh 120 U.S. tons (109 metric tons).

Dinosaurs lived throughout the Mesozoic era for 120 million years. That is longer than any other kind of land animals has ever lived, although some insects have beaten the dinosaurs' record.

Dinosaurs, more than any other prehistoric animals, have fascinated humans. But for most of human history, no one knew that they even existed. In Europe, people dug up huge bones for centuries, but they had no idea what they were. The few men who had any idea about it thought they were the remains of nameless monsters that had lived before the flood told about in the Bible. According to their beliefs, Noah took a pair of every kind of animal on earth into his ark, but he left out the monsters, and they died in the flood.

By the end of the eighteenth century, about 200 years ago, some scientifically minded men understood that the big bones were those of animals that had lived very long ago, but they had no idea how long. The young science of geology, which now makes it possible to know how long ago rocks were formed, was not yet advanced enough to do that in the eighteenth century. So those who found fossil bones had no way of finding how long ago the prehistoric animals had lived.

A little more than half a century later, scientists and amateur fossil finders, such as Baron Georges Cuvier in France and Dr. Gideon Mantell, Rev. William Buckland, and Sir Richard Owen in England, began to look at the fossil bones scientifically. They gave names to the prehistoric animals and tried to place them into their proper place among all animals. This effort led Richard Owen to decide that the animals from which certain fossil bones came were not only reptiles, but a special kind of reptiles. He gave them the name "dinosaur," which means "terrible lizard."

DINOSAURS IN AMERICA

In 1835, Edward Hitchcock was president of Amherst College and professor of theology and geology. He obtained some rocks with footprints of animals in them, and recognized them to be fossil footprints. This was the beginning of paleontology in America. For thirty years afterward, he wan-

DICINODONT

DICINODONT

CYNOGNATHUS

dered up and down the Connecticut River valley looking for more footprints in rock. He found twenty-one such places. Hitchcock thought the footprints had been made by birds. And no one knew he was wrong until a kind of dinosaur that walked on its hind legs and had birdlike feet had been discovered.

Several million years before the appearance of the first mammals, mammallike reptiles such as the Dicinodont, an herb eater, and Cynognathus, a meat eater, roamed southern Africa.

MR. FOULKE'S AND DR. LEIDY'S DINOSAUR

The first dinosaur fossils to be correctly put together into a skeleton were discovered in England more than 150 years ago. Twenty-five years later, the first discovery of a dinosaur fossil skeleton took place in this way. Workmen digging a pit at Haddonfield, New Jersey, found some very large, heavy bones. They asked, "What can these be? They're too large to be horses' bones." But the workmen could not answer their own question. They took home some of the bones, and gave them to their families and friends as curiosities.

Twenty years after that, Mr. W. Parker Foulke saw one of the curious bones from New Jersey. Being interested in nature study, he recognized that the strange object was a fossil. He then went to the farmer on whose land the pit had been dug, and got permission to dig some more. He found more fossil bones, and took them to Dr. Joseph W. Leidy, who was a professor of

SALTOPOSUCHUS

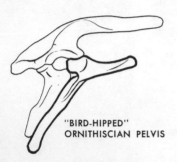

"BIRD-HIPPED"
ORNITHISCIAN PELVIS

At first all dinosaurs walked on
their hind legs. They were
divided into two groups.
Because the hip structure in
their skeletons was so different,
one group was called
lizard-hipped, and the other, a
more advanced group, was
called bird-hipped.

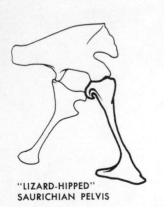

"LIZARD-HIPPED"
SAURICHIAN PELVIS

anatomy at the University of Pennsylvania, and also was on the scientific staff of the Philadelphia Academy of Natural Sciences.

Dr. Leidy studied the fossil bones and was able to put them together in proper order. But he found many bones missing. He went to New Jersey and knocked on doors in Haddonfield trying to find the missing bones. He found a few, but most were lost. However, he was able to put together most of the skeleton of a dinosaur. The one that Dr. Leidy had reconstructed was *Hadrosaurus* (had-ruh-SAWR-us), a name that means "bulky lizard."

This was the first dinosaur found in the New World. The skeleton can still be seen in the Philadelphia Academy of Natural Sciences. The name plate on it reads "Hadrosaurus foulkei," which means "hadrosaur in honor of Foulke."

The First Dinosaur

Early in the Triassic period a reptile about four feet (1¼ meters) long was running through the forests. It was *Saltoposuchus,* (sawl-toe-poe-SOOK-us). Why it was given this name is not known. It walked on its hind legs. Its forelegs were small, and were really arms. It had a long, slender body

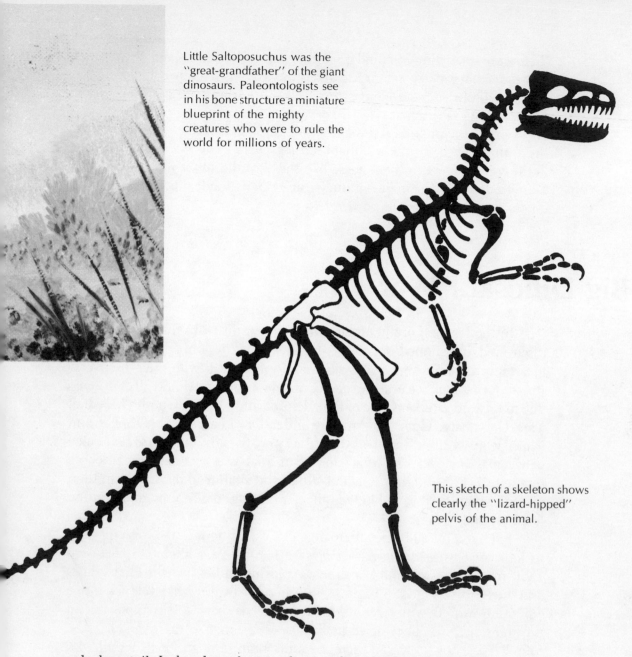

Little Saltoposuchus was the "great-grandfather" of the giant dinosaurs. Paleontologists see in his bone structure a miniature blueprint of the mighty creatures who were to rule the world for millions of years.

This sketch of a skeleton shows clearly the "lizard-hipped" pelvis of the animal.

and a long tail. Its head was long and pointed, and its jaws had needle–sharp teeth. It was the first of the dinosaurs. From Saltoposuchus all dinosaurs— even the largest—descended.

As more and more different kinds of dinosaurs appeared during the Triassic period, they split into two kinds. One kind was the *ornithischian* (orn-ith-ISS-kee-yan), or "bird-hipped dinosaurs." The other was the *saurischian* (sawr-ISS-kee-yan), or "lizard–hipped dinosaur." Among them there were small dinosaurs and giant dinosaurs, plant eaters and meat eaters, dinosaurs that walked on four legs and those that walked upright on two legs. All ornithischians were plant eaters, but there were both plant and meat eaters among saurischians.

One of the important things that made dinosaurs so successful among the animals of their time was that their legs were under their bodies. They did not extend out to their sides, like those of the other reptiles, such as Dimetrodon. Having their legs under their bodies made it possible for some dinosaurs to walk upright on two legs.

The Big Dinosaur War

In the last half of the nineteenth century, dinosaur fossils were being discovered and studied in Europe, but it was in the United States that the greatest number of dinosaur fossils were found. And, with their discovery, the study of fossils became the science of paleontology. Almost all of this was due to Edward Drinker Cope of Philadelphia and Othniel Charles Marsh of Yale University. Cope had studied under Dr. Leidy. Both Drinker and Marsh were wealthy, and at one time they were friends. But a feud developed between them over just what kind of animal was a certain long-necked reptile called Elasmosaurus (about which you shall read more). From then on, each man tried to outdo the other in finding, describing, and naming fossil animals.

Each man used his wealth to organize expeditions to the western states to look for fossils—preferrably dinosaur fossils. Year after year, between 1870 and 1895, Cope and Marsh sent exploring parties into the Plains states and the Rocky Mountain Basin. This series of expeditions developed into a "dinosaur war" in which each side tried to get as many fossils as possible in the shortest time. They acted as if there were only so many fossils to be found. We know now that there are more than enough fossils for all who look for them. But Marsh and Cope did not know this at the time.

Independent fossil explorers who knew of the feud between Cope and Marsh would hide their finds and then write to one (or even both) of the wealthy paleontologists, offering to sell their fossils. The dinosaur war became somewhat like a spy novel. The western agents of Marsh and Cope changed their names when they traveled, pretended to be salesmen or businessmen, and checked handwriting samples before they would talk to those they went to meet. At one time the war became so bitter that the exploring parties would smash the fossil bones they could not cart away. They did not want their rivals to get them.

The results of this bitter and foolish war were the two largest and most important collections of dinosaur fossils in the world. And also a great advance in the science of paleontology.

THOSE BIG NAMES

By now, you must have noticed that prehistoric animals have very long names. The names are made up of Latin and ancient Greek words that tell something about the plant or animal. Words in these two languages have the same meanings for people all over the world, no matter what their own language may be. So, scientists in all countries name animals and plants, prehistoric and modern, by using Latin and Greek words. This makes it possible for girls and boys in Japan or Argentina, Canada or India to call Brontosaurus or Allosaurus by the same name you do.

There are some exceptions to this naming rule. For example, a paleontologist named Lawrence Lambe discovered a fossil reptile, and it was named *Lambeosaurus* ("Lambe's lizard") in his honor.

Camptosaurus, a reptile of the Jurassic Period, had four toes on its hind legs and not three, as earlier dinosaurs had. Camptosaurus was a plant eater.

ALLOSAURUS

During most of the Triassic period, which lasted about 35 million years, dinosaurs did not grow very big, not much bigger than Saltoposuchus. In the period that followed, the Jurassic, they seemed to explode to gigantic size. The fiercest of the giant meat eating Jurassic dinosaurs was *Allosaurus* (al-luh-SAWR-us), whose name means "jumping lizard." It was given this name because it is believed to have jumped upon the other dinosaurs it hunted for food.

From the tip of its tail to the end of its nose it was 35 feet (10½ meters) long. Both its hind and fore legs were armed with large, sharp, hooked claws. It could grasp some of the dinosaurs it hunted with the claws of its fore legs—which were more like arms—while it tore at its victim with the claws of one of its hind legs. While doing this, it may have balanced on its tail as well as its other hind leg. Allosaurus' lower jaw was hinged to the upper jaw in a way that made it possible for this meat eater to take huge bites. And both its jaws had large sharp teeth. This dinosaur was truly a terrible killing machine.

If Allosaurus were like modern large meat eating reptiles, such as crocodiles, the dinosaur would gorge itself on the flesh of its victim. Then it would rest for several days while it digested its huge meal.

A carnivorous—meat eating—dinosaur, such as Allosaurus, is also called a *carnosaur.*

Although the first dinosaurs walked upright, like Allosaurus, many kinds of four-footed dinosaurs appeared in the late Triassic period and in the Jurassic period. All of them were plant eaters, and some of them were the largest of all dinosaurs.

THE WALKING TANK

In the Cretaceous period, a medium-sized plant eating dinosaur roamed around without much fear of any other dinosaur. It was *Ankylosaurus* (an-kyle-uh-SAWR-us), which got its name because of its very curved ribs. It was about as big as its ancestor Stegosaurus, but it was heavier and more massive. Its back was under a dome of thick bone armor. It looked somewhat like a modern tortoise. The bottom rim of the armor dome had thick spikes sticking out sideways. Ankylosaurus' head and tail were also protected by bony armor plates. On the end of the tail was a heavy bone knob. This dinosaur was a walking tank. The only part of Ankylosaurus not protected by thick armor was its belly.

It is not likely that even a carnosaur as big and powerful as Tyran-

DIPLODOCUS

ALLOSAURUS

Protected by a thick-boned armor plate from head to foot, Ankylosaurus reached a length of ten feet.

nosaurus rex would successfully attack Ankylosaurus. When it was attacked, this armored dinosaur would need only to crouch down so that its belly was close to the ground. The attacking dinosaur could not bite or tear through Ankylosaurus armor. Meanwhile, Ankylosaurus would be thrashing vigorously about with its strong tail. A blow from the knob on the end of the tail would break the leg or jaws of the attacking meat eater. If the meat eater tried to flip Ankylosaurus over to get at its belly, there were the spikes to put a stop to this. Ankylosaurus had several cousins, all of them heavily armored. Two of them had spikes on the knobs at the ends of their tails to further discourage their enemies.

HOW DINOSAURS WERE BORN

We learned that many Protoceratops' eggs have been found. They were eight inches long and half as wide. The outsides of their shells were wrinkled with ridges, except at one end. The wrinkles added strength to the shell in the same way that wrinkling cardboard makes it stronger for use in corrugated packing boxes. The ends of the eggs did not have ridges so that they would be weak enough for the baby dinosaurs to break through when they were ready to hatch.

There was a big dinosaur called *Hypselosaurus* (hip-sel-uh-SAWR-us), which means "high lizard." It was 35 feet (11 meters) long and weighed 10 U.S. tons (9 metric tons). It lived in what is now France and its eggs were discovered there. They were about twice as big as an ostrich's egg and held almost two gallons (3⅓ liters). Paleontologists think this is about as big as an egg can be. If it were bigger, gravity pulling on what is inside would cause enough pressure to break the shell. If the shell were thick enough to stand the pressure, it would be too hard or tough for the tiny hatching animal to break out of.

Could a dinosaur as big as Brontosaurus hatch from an egg no bigger than Hypselosaurus' egg? Yes, because the size of an animal when it is hatched or born does not have very much influence on how big it can grow. But did so small a newly hatched brontosaur ever exist?

One thing that is certain is that a newly hatched dinosaur could not be bigger than the egg it just hatched from. This would mean that a hatchling brontosaur was no longer than about 16 inches (41 centimeters). This is about the size of a poodle, and is less than half the length of the footprint of the baby brontosaur's mother. How could such a tiny brontosaur keep from being stepped on as it wandered among the huge feet of a herd of brontosaurs? It probably could not. So, it is likely that brontosaurs—and other giant dinosaurs—were *ovoviviparous* (o-vo-viv-IP-ur-us). This means that the mother dinosaur did not lay eggs, but kept them inside her body until they hatched. Then, the baby dinosaurs were born alive. They may have been as big as full grown horses when they were born. Some modern lizards and snakes are ovoviviparus.

One reason to believe that many kinds of dinosaurs were ovoviviparus is that a large number of dinosaur fossils have been found, but very few dinosaur eggs have been discovered.

So, then, some dinosaurs were hatched from buried eggs, and some were hatched from eggs inside their mothers and born alive.

The photo shows Protoceratops with eggs. It was taken from a reconstruction in the Museum of Natural History in New York.

BRONTOSAURUS

American Indians who lived in the Southwest many years ago now and then found huge fossil bones. These were bigger than bones of any animal the Indians knew of—bigger even than bones of a bison. The Indians decided that the bones came from "thunder horses" that leaped down from the sky to earth during thunderstorms. A scientist who knew of the Indian legend and knew also that some of the bones were those of a dinosaur, named it *Brontosaurus* (bron-tuh-SAWR-us), meaning "thunder lizard." Unfortunately, other scientists had already given this dinosaur the name *Apatosaurus* (a-pat-uh-SAWR-us). However, this name was given before there were rules for naming prehistoric animals, and no one now knows what it means. In this book, we shall use the name Brontosaurus.

This dinosaur weighed more than 30 U.S. tons (35 metric tons). It stood on four legs, each as wide as a doorway—39 inches (one meter). Its hind legs were longer than its fore legs, causing its back to slope down from rear to front. Each foot had pads on the bottom, like those on the feet of elephants. There were large toenails on four of its five toes. The inside toes ended in big, sharp claws. We do not know how they were used—maybe for ripping up the trunks of trees. Brontosaurus had a long, heavy tail that tapered off to a thin end.

Brontosaurus's long neck enabled it to browse on the tops of tree ferns, 30 feet (9 meters) high. Its head was no wider than the top of its neck. In its mouth were uneven, peglike teeth. Since these teeth were not made for chewing, Brontosaurus must have swallowed whole the leaves, twigs, and even branches it tore from trees. It needed a ton of this food every day. If Brontosaurus saw some delicious-looking leaves that were too high on a tree to reach, this huge dinosaur might lean its great body on the tree, bending it to the ground. Then it could easily feast on the leaves. How did Brontosaurus digest the vast amount of coarse food it ate every day? Fairly large, smooth stones have been found along with brontosaur fossils. These may have been *gastroliths* (GASS-tro-liths), stones that the dinosaur swallowed to grind up its food, as its stomach made churning motions. (Similarly, birds, lacking teeth, swallow stones to grind up their food.)

Brontosaurus lived near swamps and lakes. Its body was just about light enough to float. Some paleontologists believe this gigantic dinosaur could paddle through water that was over its back, or in shallow water that did not reach over its back.

Brontosaurs lived in herds. The only enemies they had to fear were allosaurs. A single allosaur could not kill a brontosaur anymore than a lion

can kill an elephant. Three or four allosaurs probably hung around the edges of a herd of brontosaurs. The allosaurs did not dare to attack a brontosaur herd. If they had, the frightened and angry brontosaurs, milling their gigantic bodies around in panic, swinging their long necks and huge tails, would have knocked some of the allosaurs to the ground and trampled them to death. Instead, the allosaurs probably waited for an opportunity to pounce upon a member of the herd that wandered off alone to an especially delicious-looking tree. Or, to catch a sick or old brontosaur that lagged behind the herd. Or, perhaps to catch a half-grown young brontosaur that strayed from the herd.

BRACHIOSAURUS

Brachiosaurus (brak-ee-uh-SAWR-us) is the largest dinosaur whose whole skeleton we have. Its name means "arm lizard" and it got this name because of the great size of its fore leg, which scientists first thought to be an arm.

Brachiosaurus weighed 50 U.S. tons, or 45 metric tons. It stood on four huge legs, the fore ones being longer than the hind ones. This made its back slope rearward. It was 80 feet (24 meters) long, and was tall enough to look into a third floor window.

This dinosaur had a dome of bone between its eyes. In the dome were its nostrils. Some scientists have reasoned that Brachiosaurus lived in swamps, spending much time in deep water. The bony dome enabled it to poke just the top of its head above water and still breathe. Other scientists, as we read earlier, do not believe this dinosaur lived in water, but they have no explanation for the dome.

In 1972 an American paleontologist, Dr. James Jensen, found dinosaur shoulder and neck bones that were larger than any ever found before. He gave the huge animal to whom the bones belonged the temporary name

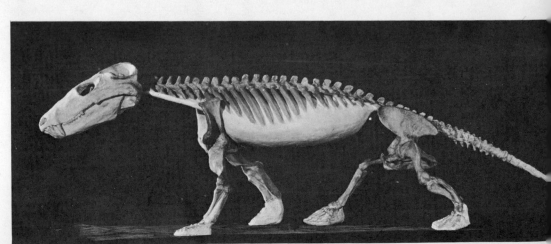

CYNOGNATHUS

34

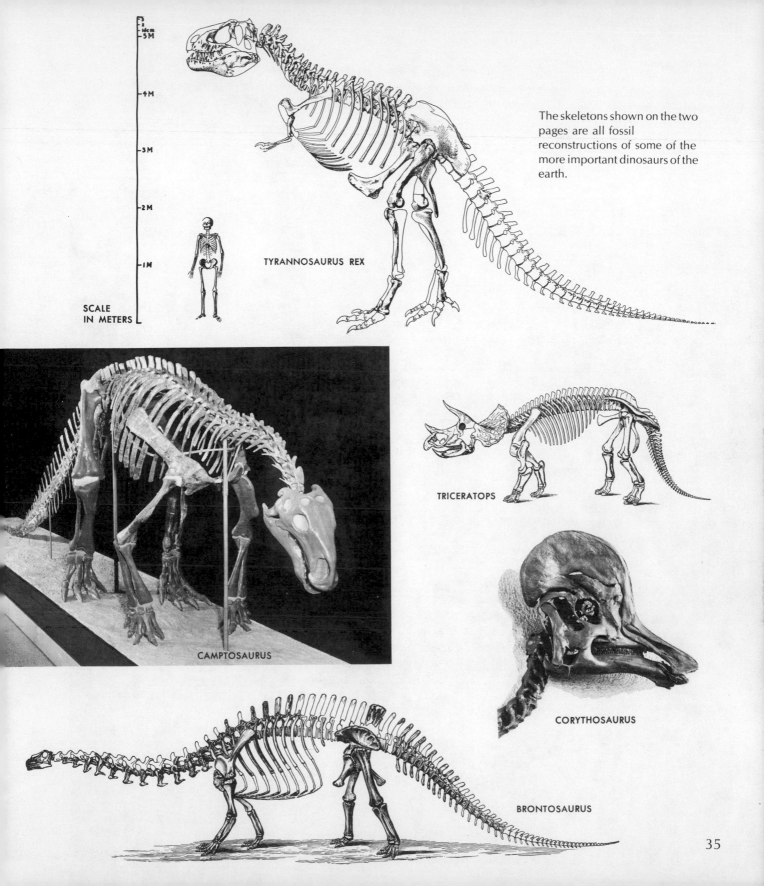

SCALE
IN METERS

TYRANNOSAURUS REX

The skeletons shown on the two pages are all fossil reconstructions of some of the more important dinosaurs of the earth.

CAMPTOSAURUS

TRICERATOPS

CORYTHOSAURUS

BRONTOSAURUS

35

BRACHIOSAURUS

Supersaurus. Seven years later, Dr. Jensen dug up an even larger shoulder bone and gave its owner the name *Ultrasaurus*. When the rest of the bones are found, we probably will see that their owners were even more gigantic than Brachiosaurus.

Besides these huge bones, there are other signs of dinosaurs larger than any yet found. For example, some coal miners in Utah once saw some gigantic footprints on the ceiling of a tunnel they were digging. They looked like the tracks of a giant bird. They were 44 inches (112 centimeters) long and 32 inches (81 centimeters) wide. The distance between each footprint was 15 feet (4½ meters). The miners reported the footprints to scientists, who came to look at them.

These scientists recognized that the footprints had been made by a dinosaur that walked on its hind legs.

The biggest known dinosaur that walked on its hind legs had a stride of nine feet (3 meters) and was 20 feet (6 meters) tall. So, a dinosaur with a stride as big as those on the ceiling of the mine tunnel would probably have been 35 feet (11 meters) tall.

The same kind of footprints have also been found in Colorado, but no parts of fossil bones that might go with them have been discovered. So, we have no idea of what the dinosaur that made the ceiling footprints looked like.

How could footprints of a huge dinosaur come to be on the ceiling of an underground tunnel? The dinosaur probably walked in thick mud, leaving its footprints. The mud was on top of a bed of coal. Sand blew onto the mud, filling the footprints and covering them hundreds of feet deep. Millions of years later, the mud and sand had turned to rock. The miners were digging coal at an underground level below the footprints. So, when they dug their tunnel, they uncovered the footprints on the tunnel's ceiling.

While we are talking about dinosaur size, there is an interesting fact to learn. Unlike other kinds of animals, reptiles never stop growing. Most of the animals you know about—dog, cats, horses, elephants, whales, humans—grow rapidly when they are young. When they reach a certain age, they stop. Reptiles keep on growing, although they increase in size more and more slowly as they get older. Dinosaurs, too, may have continued to grow all through their lives.

DIPLODOCUS

Brontosaurus and Brachiosaurus had a very long cousin named *Diplodocus* (dip-LAH-duh-cus), or "double beam." It was given this name because each of the vertebraes that made up its backbone had a double spike, or beam. Diplodocus was more than 97 feet (30 meters) long, but its body was slimmer than those of its immense cousins. Its neck was just about as long as its tail. Its small head was no wider than its neck, and it had many long, pencil-like teeth. Diplodocus, like the other long-necked, plant eating dinosaurs, held its head high so that it could browse on leaves and twigs of trees. It had the smallest brain of all the big plant eaters.

Diplodocus is probably the best known of all dinosaurs. There is a good reason for this. The first skeleton of this dinosaur to be discovered was put together and displayed in the museum of the Carnegie Institute in Pittsburgh in 1895. Ten years later, the British king, Edward VII, was visiting Andrew Carnegie, the man who built the Carnegie Institute and had Diplodocus put into its museum. The king said he hoped that someday the British Museum would have a monster skeleton such as the one of Diplodocus. Carnegie immediately gave orders to make a model of the dinosaur out of plaster, and had it shipped to the British Museum. It made such a hit that Carnegie had other models of Diplodocus sent to museums in Paris, Berlin, Vienna, Bologna, Mexico City, and to La Plata, in Argentina. Smaller models were sent to many other museums. With so many models of its skeletons on view in so many places, it is no wonder that Diplodocus is the most famous dinosaur. (For illustration, see page 29.)

Water or Land?

Did Diplodocus and its other colossal cousins live on land or in water? For a long time, paleontologists believed that these plant eating dinosaurs lived in water—swamps and lakes. In the water, they were safe from the large meat eaters such as Allosaurus. These enemies could not swim nor wade in water as deep as that where the plant eaters lived and fed on water plants.

Also, the scientists said, there is a limit to the strength of bones. The giant plant eaters were so heavy they needed the support that water gave them. If they had walked on land, their great weight would break their bones and tear their muscles, intestines, and other internal organs.

Other paleontologists say these things are not true. The giant plant eaters could walk on land because they had bones that were light, yet strong enough to support their monstrous weight. Also, if they stood in deep water, with only their heads above the surface to breathe, the pressure of the water on their bodies would have been so great that breathing would be impossible. What is more, the big dinosaurs could not escape meat eaters by fleeing into the water, because that is where giant crocodiles with six foot (2 meter) jaws lived.

Still other paleontologists say that the big plant eaters wandered in and out of water, as they fed on water or land plants. And they could move fast enough to flee into water deep enough to be safe from land-living meat eaters.

The paleontologists' debate about the giant dinosaurs' living in water or on land is not over.

THE DUCKBILLS

Camptosaurus (kamp-tuh-SAWR-us) means "bent lizard." It was called that because some of the time it walked on its two hind legs, bent over from its hips. At other times it walked on all fours, using its smaller front legs. It was about 7 feet (2 meters) long. (See illustration on page 27.)

Camptosaurus had a horny ducklike beak that it used for cutting and biting off the plants that were its food. Behind the beak were flattened bladelike teeth for chewing the plants. Camptosaurus was the first of a line of dinosaurus called "duckbills." Two of its descendants were Iguanodon and Trachodon.

At just about the time that Camptosaurus appeared, the Jurassic period ended. It had been a time—55 million years long—during which dinosaurs changed from small reptiles darting through the tropical forests of the Mesozoic era to gigantic animals lumbering through the swamps and being hunted by other huge dinosaurs with terrifying teeth and claws. Dinosaurs ruled all the animals of the earth.

STEGOSAURUS

A large bird-hipped dinosaur, *Stegosaurus* (steg-o-SAWR-us), appeared about the middle of the Jurassic period. Its name means "covered lizard" and refers to the strange natural armor with which it was covered. Along the middle of its back, it had two rows of horny plates. What good were the plates? They undoubtedly made it hard for meat eating dinosaurs to attack Stegosaurus. They also may have been a cooling organ, like the sail of Dimetrodon.

Stegosaurus' tail had five long, sharp spikes. When Allosaurus attacked, Stegosaurus would crouch down, leaning to one side, and lash out with its strong, spiked tail. This defense must have worked because Stegosaurus and the towering meat eaters lived alongside each other for millions of years.

Stegosaurus' fore legs were so much shorter than its hind legs that its nose almost touched the ground. Its teeth were fitted for cutting and grinding tough plants. So, it could wander inland, away from the soft plants that grew in swamps and near lakes.

Stegosaurus was 20 feet (6 meters) long and about 10 feet (3 meters) high—a big animal. It weighed 10 U.S. tons (9 metric tons) yet its brain was no larger than a walnut. Above its hips, its spinal cord was enlarged. This enlargement is sometimes spoken of as a second brain. But it was probably a big bundle of nerves, or a special gland that helped the small brain when the animal was in danger.

IGUANODON

Dr. Gideon Mantell, an English physician, was more interested in fossils than medicine. His wife, too, was interested in fossils. One morning in March 1822, in Sussex, she was waiting for her husband who was visiting a patient. At a place where a road was being repaved, she found a few large fossil teeth. Neither she nor her husband could figure out what kind of animal the teeth came from. Dr. Mantell sent them to Baron Georges Cuvier, a famous French naturalist. Cuvier decided the teeth had belonged to a rhinoceros. This did not satisfy Mantell, who returned to where the teeth had been found, and dug up some fossil bones that probably belonged to the same animal. Baron Cuvier now decided the bones and teeth were those of a hippopotamus. Dr. Mantell still was not satisfied. After careful study, he decided the fossils came from a prehistoric reptile much like the iguana lizard, that lives today in tropical America, the West Indies, and some Pacific Ocean islands. So, he named the prehistoric owner of the fossil teeth and bones, *Iguanodon* (i-GWAN-uh-don), meaning "iguana-like tooth." It was not called a dinosaur because that word had not yet been coined.

The Iguanodon was a duck-billed dinosaur, about as long as Allosaurus (30 feet, or 9 meters), but it was bulkier, weighing 6½ U.S. tons (6 metric tons), to the Allosaurs' 4½ U.S. tons (4 metric tons). It walked on its two hind legs most of the time, but Dr. Mantell did not know this. He put the Iguanodon's skeleton together as if it were a four-footed animal. This was considered to be its correct posture for many years, until thirty-one fossil Iguanodons were found in the walls of a Belgian coal mine. These gave paleontologists enough information to realize that Iguanodon usually walked on only two legs.

STEGOSAURUS

The finding of the Iguanodons in the coal mine was an amazing experience for the paleontologists who dug them out. The mine was at Bernissart. Here, 180 million years after coal had formed, some movement in the earth's crust, perhaps an earthquake, opened a deep ravine in the coal. Then, thirty-one Iguanodons fell into the ravine. How did so many of these dinosaurs fall over a cliff, all at the same time? Did the earthquake that made the ravine frighten a herd of Iguanodons so much that they panicked and all ran over the cliff, one after another? Did a pack of Allosaurs chase the herd off the cliff? Or, did a flash flood drown the Iguanodons and wash them into the ravine? We will never know, but we do know that the ravine filled with mud and buried the Iguanodons. When mud slowly turned into a kind of rock called marl, the Iguanodons turned into fossils.

A Belgian paleontologist, Louis Dollo, spent most of his life getting the Iguanodon fossils out of the mine, removing them from the surrounding rock, and setting them up in the Brussels Royal Museum of Natural History. He had the idea that when Iguanodons grew very old and weak, they wandered off to a place to die. One such graveyard, Dollo thought, was the Bernissart ravine. He may have gotten this idea from an old false belief that elephants have graveyards.

The Iguanadon got its name because the fossil teeth resemble those of the iguana lizard that lives today in tropical America.

DINOSAURS' TAILS

Almost all dinosaurs had long tails. How did they hold them? For a long time paleontologists pictured the tails resting on the ground. Those dinosaurs that stood upright, such as Allosaurus, leaned back on their tails when standing still. When running, they lifted their tails off the ground. The big plant eaters, such as Brontosaurus, dragged their tails as they lumbered along.

When more dinosaur skeletons were studied, some scientists changed their ideas. They decided that a two-legged dinosaur did not stand erect as had been thought. It leaned far forward, the front of its body balancing its tail, which could be held straight out. The way the tail bones were formed seems to show that there was stiff cartilage between them. This made it possible for the tails to be held straight back, off the ground.

The dinosaurs that walked on four legs, simply held their tails straight out behind them. In those few places where footprints of dinosaurs have been found there are no tracks made by dragging tails. A hundred million years ago, near what is now Glen Rose, Texas, there was a beach of lime mud, which turned into limestone. A brontosaur left its huge footprints in the mud. Not long afterward, an allosaur, that was following the brontosaur, also left its tracks. But there are no traces in the mud of either of these dinosaurs' tails. So they must have been held in the air.

For most paleontologists, it is not hard to agree with the newer idea that dinosaurs such as Allosaurus held their tails off the ground most of the time. But it is hard to believe that the same is true for Brontosaurus and its big cousins. These scientists point out that nature is very good at saving energy. And it would waste a lot of energy for a dinosaur to hold a tail weighing several tons off the ground most of the time. So, to answer the argument about the lack of fossil tail tracks: lime mud is usually covered by shallow water, so the dinosaurs' tails would have floated in the water above the mud, leaving no tracks.

TRACHODON

The dinosaur, Hadrosaurus, that Mr. Foulke and Dr. Leidy put into the Philadelphia museum is a duckbill better known by the name, Trachodon (TRAK-uh-don). The name means "rough tooth," and describes this dinosaur's many teeth which formed a rough sort of pavement in its mouth. Each side of each jaw had more than 500 teeth for a total of 2000. Trachodon had a flat head, and the front of its mouth looked so very much like a duck's bill that this feature gave these dinosaurs the nickname "duckbills." They are also known by the scientific names, *trachodonts*, or *hadrosaurs*.

Trachodon was a big dinosaur, 35 feet (11 meters) long, and weighing more than 6 U.S. tons (5½ metric tons). It walked upright on its hind legs, but it had fairly long fore legs, and also walked on all fours. Trachodon's fossilized footprints show that it had big toes, and between them were thick, leathery webs. The fossils of hadrosaurs are very often found along with the fossils of crocodiles, garfish, turtles and other animals that lived in water. So, some paleontologists say that the duckbills were waders and swimmers. Other scientists say duckbills did not live near water, because their teeth show they ate leaves of trees that grew only in the dry highlands, not soft plants that grew in marshes.

Many kinds of trachodonts had hollow, bony crests on their heads. The crests had very unusual shapes.

All these bony crests were hollow and connected with the dinosaurs' nasal passages. They may have been used to increase the loudness (as the curves and horn of a trombone do) of whatever sounds trachodonts made. Or, perhaps the crests had the same kind of lining our noses have. If this were so, it would have increased the sharpness of the duckbills' sense of smell. This would have warned them of the presence of meat eaters in time to flee. Duckbills needed early warning because they had no claws or big teeth with which to fight their enemies. All they could do was run away.

Artist's conception of a Trachodon, the first dinosaur skeleton discovered in the United States. Having as many as 2,000 teeth in his duck bill, he probably rooted after his food in much the same manner as a duck does. His webbed feet may have helped him in swimming, and his ability to take to the water may have served as protection against dinosaur-eating enemies. Trachodon lived during the Mesozoic Era, 170,000,000 years ago.

TRACHODON

Styracosaurus, a plant eater, lived during the Upper Cretaceous period, about 90 million years ago.

THE FRILLED DINOSAURS

In the last half of the Cretaceous period there lived a family of plant eating dinosaurs called *ceratopsians* (ser-uh-TOPS-ee-uns), which means "horn faces."

The first of these dinosaurs lived in what is now Mongolia. It was *Protoceratops* (pro-toe-SER-uh-tops), which means—as you can guess—"first horn face." As dinosaurs go, this one was small, being five to six feet long and walking on four short legs. Its horn was very small; it was just a bump halfway between the eyes and nostrils. Protoceratops had a large head. In its mouth were only two small teeth. At the front of its skull was a hooked, parrot-like beak. A broad bony collar, or "frill," on either side of its head below each eye, covered its neck, and extended halfway down its back. This collar was an anchor for the strong muscles it needed to control the movements of its big head. It also may have been a defense against meat eaters which killed their prey by clamping their jaws around its neck. If a meat eater that pounced on Protoceratops could not successfully bite through its neck because of the collar, then the plant eater may have had a second chance to run away.

Several nests of fossil Protoceratops' eggs have been found. They were the first known dinosaur eggs and were discovered in Mongolia about sixty years ago. They probably had leathery shells, like the eggs of modern turtles. In two of the Protoceratops' eggs were found the bones of unhatched young dinosaurs. The female Protoceratops laid her eggs in a shallow hole scraped in the ground. She then covered them with earth. Unlike almost all modern reptiles, she did not abandon her eggs, but stayed nearby until the warmth of the sun hatched them.

A large number of fossil skeletons of Protoceratops have been dug up. We have a series of them that reveal how Protoceratops looked from the time it was in the egg until it was an adult. One thing they show is that the newly-hatched dinosaurs had only a small bony collar, but it grew as they grew.

One of Protoceratops' descendants was *Monoclonius* (mono-KLON-e-us), which means "single stem." This refers to the large horn in the center of its skull, just behind its nose. It also had two very short stubby horns over its eyes. Its bony frill had a scalloped edge. Except for the frill and the stubby horns, Monoclonius looked much like a modern rhinocerus.

A descendant of Monoclonius was *Styracosaurus* (sty-rak-uh-SAWR-us), whose name means "spike lizard." It was much bigger than its ancestors, being 30 feet (9 meters) long and 10 feet (3 meters) high. It weighed more than 10 U.S. tons (9 metric tons). Its head, including the frill, was almost eight feet (2½ meters) long. Its horns were like those of Monoclonius.

Triceratops, a plant eater, was far from being a gentle animal and even knew how to defend itself against the mighty Tyrannosaurus rex.

Instead of being scalloped, its bony frill had six long spikes that stuck out from the upper edge.

A cousin of Styracosaurus that lived at the same time was *Triceratops* (try-SER-uh-tops), whose name means "three horn face." It was a little larger than its cousin. The edge of its bony frill was smooth, having no scallops or spikes. Its horns were the reverse of those on the head of Styracosaurus. There was a small stumpy one not far behind Triceratops' beak, and two very long sharp ones above its eyes. The big horns pointed forward and stuck out past the end of its nose. They were three to four feet (1 to 1¼ meters) long. Triceratops' hind legs were longer than its fore legs, so its head always was lowered, as though it were ready to attack with its horns.

Triceratops traveled in vast herds. When attacked by a big carnosaur, a group of Triceratops would form a circle with their young in the center. Faced by the circle of long horns, backed by powerful neck muscles, the meat eater may have paid dearly—even with its life—for the attack. Forming a circle for defense took a fair amount of intelligence, and Triceratops was the smartest of the dinosaurs. Its brain weighed two pounds (900 grams). This was about a dozen times more than the brain of any other dinosaur.

Recently, some paleontologists have concluded that the large bony collars were not above the necks of the ceratopsians. Instead, they were surrounded by the neck muscles, for which they were anchors. So, of course, the collars were under the dinosaurs' skins and could not be seen. If this idea is correct, the scientists will have to come up with a whole new shape for the heads and shoulders of the ceratopsians. It is possible that these dinosaurs had big humps behind their heads.

THE BONEHEADED DINOSAUR

There was one dinosaur that was a real bonehead. It was *Pachycephalosaurus* (pak-ee-SEF-uh-lo-sawr-us), which means "bonehead lizard." It was a relative of the duckbills, but it did not develop the hollow crest and flat bill of its relatives. Instead, it had a thick solid dome of bone on its head and a blunt, warty face with small, blunt horns. Its bony dome was nine inches (23 centimeters) thick. Within it was a tiny brain. Paleontologists do not know of what use the bony head was. They guess that males may have butted their heads together in contests for the favor of female pachycephalosaurs during the mating season. It may have butted its enemies very hard with its head, but it could hardly have beaten a meat eater such as Tyrannosaurus rex, which lived at the same time as Pachycephalosaurus.

The plant eating dinosaurs of the Jurassic period had to fear Allosaurus and its slightly smaller carnosaur cousins. But the plant eaters of the Cretaceous period faced an even more terrible dinosaur. It was *Tyrannosaurus* (tye-ran-uh-SAWR-us), or "tyrant lizard." A tyrant is a cruel ruler who will allow no one to do anything against him in any way. Paleontologists consider Tyrannosaurus to have been a tyrant over all the other dinosaurs—the most fearsome animal that nature ever created. They back up their opinion of this dinosaur by adding to its name the word "rex," which means "king." Tyrannosaurus rex truly was the "tyrant lizard king." But it is usually called simply Tyrannosaurus.

It was bigger and heavier than Allosaurus, being 20 feet (6 meters) tall

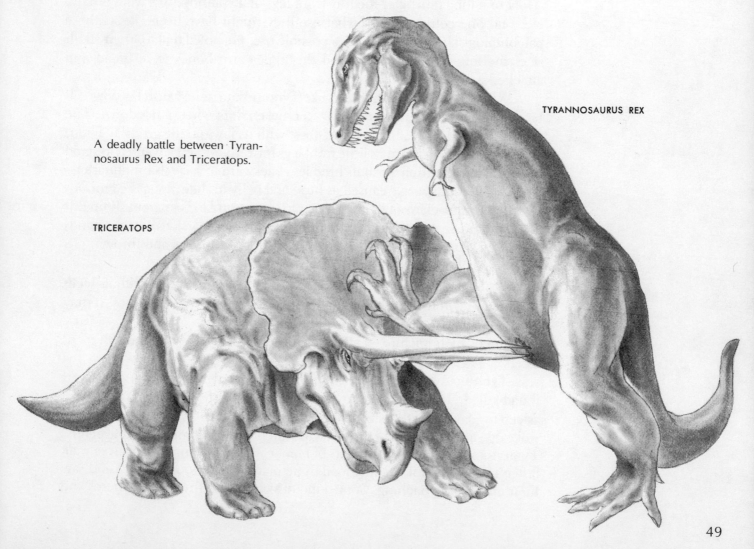

TYRANNOSAURUS REX

A deadly battle between Tyrannosaurus Rex and Triceratops.

TRICERATOPS

and 48 feet (15 meters) long from its nose to the tip of its tail, and it weighed eight tons (7 metric tons). Its head was more than four feet (1¼ meters) long. Many of its sharp teeth were more than six inches (15 centimeters) long and curved inward, so that it could get a firm grip on its prey. If it broke any of its teeth, it grew new ones to replace them. It could tear off more than 50 pounds (23 kilograms) of flesh in a single bite. It could gorge itself on a quarter of a ton (225 kilograms) of meat at a single meal.

Tyrannosaurus had three toes on each of its two birdlike feet, and each toe had a long, sharp claw. This dinosaur's forelimbs, or arms, were so short they could not reach to its mouth. They were only about thirty inches long—shorter than the arms of many humans. Tyrannosaurus could not—as Allosaurus could—use its forelimbs to grasp a dinosaur it was attacking.

For a long time after the tiny front legs of Tyrannosaurus were discovered, no one could think of what use they might have been. Recently, a paleontologist has come up with a possible use. He noted that for their small size, the legs had big claws. And the upper arm bones were broad and attached to strong shoulder bones.

When a two-legged dinosaur like Tyrannosaurus rested, it lay down. It tucked its hind legs under its body as a chicken does when it lies down. The dinosaur rested its head, as a lizard does, with its jaws on the ground. Then, Tyrannosaurus stretched its little front legs forward. When it wanted to stand up, it could not simply push its hind legs backward to raise its hindquarters. This would merely have caused its head and belly to slide along the ground. So it dug the big claws of its front legs into the ground to keep from sliding. It could now raise its hindquarters off the ground, as a cow does when it stands up. Then, pushing up with its tiny, but strong, front legs and throwing its head back, it could, at last, stand up.

When Tyrannosaurus attacked, it tried to grasp its victim with its teeth and rip at it with the claws of one foot. As it stood on the other foot, it may have used its large tail to balance itself.

Let us try to picture an attack by Tyrannosaurus rex on a herd of plant eaters.

Tyrannosaurus had eaten an immense amount of flesh from a dinosaur it had killed. Then it had gone into the forest to rest. It had been lying half asleep for days, as it digested its huge meal. But now it was hungry again. It woke up and walked out of the forest in search of its next meal. On the plains, Tyrannosaurus saw vast numbers of plant eating dinosaurs. It began to walk faster and faster as it smelled food. The plant eaters, too, smelled and saw their enemy approaching. Some kind of signal went through the herds and all their members stopped eating. Some fled, others watched warily. Tyrannosaurus had picked out the dinosaurs it wanted to kill. It began to run in great 15-foot (4½ meter) strides toward a herd of Triceratops. The herd had formed a circle with the young in the center. When Tyrannosaurus reached the circle, it tried to break through to get at the young Triceratops within. But one of the adults turned with surprising swiftness and gored Tyrannosaurus leg with both of its horns. Tyrannosaurus stumbled and the next Triceratops in the circle made a rip in Tyrannosaurus' side. But the carnosaur was on its feet in a second and attacked the first Triceratops. With a clawed foot, Tyrannosaurus ripped at its victim. Then, closing in, it bit through the tough hide and into Triceratops backbone. The dying plant eater was able to turn, and with one horn, pierce Tyrannosaurus' other side. The rest of the herd panicked and ran.

Although very badly wounded, Tyrannosaurus began to tear great chunks of flesh out of its victim. Not long afterward, Tyrannosaurus, too, died.

Another Tyrannosaurus, having smelled the blood of the mortal struggle between the two dinosaurs, came up to their corpses and began to gorge itself upon them.

Reptiles of the Seas

While thirty ton dinosaurs lumbered through marshes and over plains, very big reptiles swam in the seas. At the same time that reptiles dominated the land, they also ruled the seas. It was an Age of Reptiles both on land and in the water.

Three times during the Mesozoic era, the ocean flowed over North America, making inland seas. When they were largest, they spread from the Allegheny to the Rocky Mountains. These seas were shallow when compared to the Atlantic or Pacific Oceans.

Although reptiles first appear in the fossil record as land animals, some of them went to live in the seas, along with their distant ancestors, the fish. This same kind of change happened with mammals, which began on land and then lost some of their numbers to the seas. Today, porpoises, whales, and seals are some of the sea-living mammals.

Paleontologists are not certain just how land animals change to sea animals. But when they do, they take on the shapes of fish. The reptiles that went to live in the seas developed fish-like bodies—without scales. Reptile tails took on the shape of fish's tails. Instead of fins, the reptiles' forelimbs and hindlimbs became flippers, which were placed on their bodies where fins are on fish's bodies. But the sea reptiles kept their lungs, never returning to the gills of their fish ancestors. Gills make it possible for fish to live entirely under water, but reptiles must rise to the surface every so often to breathe air.

The Girl and the Sea Serpent

In the last year of the eighteenth century, an English girl, Mary Anning, was born in the town of Lyme Regis, along the English seacoast. Her father, Richard, kept a shop in which he sold fossil seashells that he dug out of the chalk and slate cliffs that bordered the sea. Mary learned to help her father in his shop, and she went with him when he hunted for fossils.

When Mary was ten, her father died. She carried on his work of finding and selling fossil seashells. Two years later, she found in a blue slate cliff a skeleton of a large animal. It was almost seven feet (2 meters) long. She had to get the help of workmen to remove from the cliff the chunks of rock in which it was buried. Mary sold the large fossil to the lord of a nearby manor. He gave it to scientists for study. At that time there was no science of paleontology and the scientists were very puzzled by the fossil. It seemed to have the backbone of a fish, the skull of a lizard with extra large eye sockets, flippers (or paddles) like those of a whale and teeth of a crocodile set in a long beak.

Artist's conception of Plesiosauri chasing after food.

The scientists spent almost seven years figuring out just how the "sea serpent" (as some people called the animal) had been constructed. One problem was the appearance of its tail. A backbone is made up of a number of small, thick bone discs, called vertebras, strung together in a line. The hindmost twenty-odd vertebras of the fossil were bent sharply downward. This caused Richard Owen (the scientist who coined the word "dinosaur") to decide that the tail was broken. He also decided that the "sea serpent" had a large tail, because on the backbone there were scars where strong muscles for moving a tail had been attached. Later, after several fossil skeletons of the same animal were found, it turned out that Owen was right about the large tail. But he also was wrong—the tail had not been broken. The backbone curved sharply downward naturally. It stiffened the lower half of a flat tail, like a dolphin's. The upper half was stiffened by cartilage.

A big problem was the outer shape of the animal. Its flesh and skin left no fossil remains. Several years after Mary Anning's find, a scientist was working on another fossil of the same kind. He was trying to free the skeleton from the slab of rock in which it was found. He accidentally spilled a glass of water on the rock. When he had wiped up the water, he saw—on the rock a faint outline of the whole animal. It was shaped like a fish, having no neck, but instead a smooth, streamlined form from head to tail.

The combination of fish like and lizard like features caused the fossil sea reptile to be named *Icthyosaurus* (ik-thee-uh-SAWR-us), or "fish lizard."

Later, inside some icthyosaur fossils were found eggs with unhatched baby icthyosaurs. This meant that these sea reptiles were ovovivaporous. Land reptiles could dig shallow nests in mud or sand for their eggs. But sea reptiles could not dig nests in water. They had to be ovovivaporous.

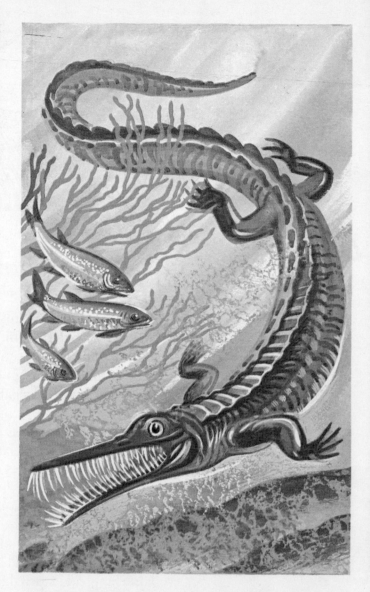

125 million years after the Silurian age, during the Permian age of the world, fish-like reptiles shared the seas with the fish. Sea-reptiles like the ferocious Sea Lizard shown above, already had made the return trip from land-living to sea-dwelling. They looked like today's crocodiles, but were only about 30 inches long. In spite of the superficial likeness to crocodiles, they are not their ancestors.

SKELETON OF A SEA REPTILE

When Icthyosaurus was finally described it was found to have looked much like a large dolphin. One exception was that it had four flippers on the lower part of its body, one on each side near the head, and one on each side near the tail. A dolphin has only two which are near its head. Icthyosaurus flippers were used for balance as its powerful tail drove it through the water. And, like a dolphin, it had on the top of its back a shark like fin, also to help balance it. Its beak was almost as long and thin as a swordfish's beak. The beak was armed with a large number of sharp teeth. It had large eyes and may have hunted by sharp eyesight.

The discovery of the Icthyosaurus fossil made Mary Anning famous in scientific circles. She followed this discovery with one of another sea reptile. It was *Plesiosaurus* (plees-ee-uh-SAWR-us), which means "near lizard." It was first thought that plesiosaurs were closely related to lizards.

These reptiles had broad bodies about as flat as turtles. Their tails were fairly long, and tapered to an end. They did not spread out and flatten, as the icthyosaurs' tails did. They had four large flippers. The most remarkable thing about them was their very snakelike necks—as long as their bodies and tails together. At the end of the neck was a small head whose jaws were studded with long sharp teeth.

Plesiosaurs were fish eaters. Instead of driving swiftly through the water in search of fish, as the icthyosaurs did, plesiosaurs probably paddled along at or near the surface of the sea, searching for fish. When a plesiosaur spied fish, it darted its long neck at them and snatched them out of the water.

The Dutch Reptile

In 1780, workmen in a sandstone quarry near Maastricht, Holland, found a large skeleton. Dr. Hofman, a French army surgeon who had previously collected fossils in the quarry, was told about the new find. He immediately came to Maastricht and removed the fossil. But a Dr. Goddin, who owned the lands above the quarry, claimed the fossil and went to court about it. The court gave it to him.

Fourteen years later, the French army was invading Holland. Maastrict was bombarded by French canon, but the suburb of Pietersberg, where Dr. Goddin lived, was spared. He guessed that the French army had orders to capture his fossil, so he hid it. For a while after the Dutch surrendered, the French could not find it. But a reward of 600 bottles of wine was offered for the skeleton. Soon, some French soldiers appeared with the fossil, which was shipped to Paris.

The skeleton was that of a *Mososaurus* (mo-so-SAWR-us), a name that means "Meuse (a river in Belgium) lizard." These reptiles never changed to a really fishlike form, but retained their long, sinuous, lizardlike bodies. They had four large flippers and a pointed head with jaws containing long, sharp teeth. Mososaurs were fish eaters. They lived in the shallow seas of North America as well as those of Europe.

Ichthyosaurus, as much as it resembles a fish, was a true reptile. It first lived on land, and then went to the sea in the course of its development, spanning millions of years.

RHAMPHORHYNCHUS

PTERANODON

ORNITHOLESTES

Flying Reptiles

When the Mesozoic era was about one-third over, a new kind of animal could be seen in the sky. It was a flying reptile. There were several different kinds, and they are called *pterosaurs* (ter-uh-SAWRS), or "winged lizards." Some of them eventually became the largest flying animals that ever lived, having a wing span of 50 feet (15 meters). Some were as small as sparrows.

One of the first of these was *Rhamphorynchus* (ram-fo-RINK-us),

ARCHAEOPTERYX

HESPERORNIS

ICHTHYORNIS

which means "prow beak." The front of its long skull was a beak, that had many long forward-pointing teeth, which Rhamphorynchus used to catch and hold the fish it ate.

It had a small body, about the size of a pigeon, and a straight, bony rod with a paddle on the end for a tail. It was about 1½ feet (½ meter) long. Each of its wings was eight feet (2½ meters) long and was made of skinlike membrane. The front of each wing was attached to a long, jointed bone, which was the fourth, or "pinkie," finger of a reptile's "hand." Rhamphorynchus's wing has always been pictured as stretching from its shoulders to its feet. But modern paleontologists point out that there is no real evidence for this. Its bones were hollow, filled with air, and very light.

Also, Rhamphorynchus has always been described as being unable to flap its wings, but only to soar and glide. However, it had strong upper arm bones and also a large breast bone and keel, which could have anchored strong muscles used for flapping its wings.

At the front of each of Rhamphorynchus's wings were three clawed fingers and a clawed thumb. It may have used these to hang from cliffs when it rested, as bats hang from the walls and ceilings of caves.

Sixty million years after Rhamphorynchus soared over the seas that were where Central Europe is now, other, larger pterosaurs glided or flew above the seas that covered the middle of North America. One of them was *Pteranodon* (ter-AN-uh-don), or "wing without teeth." This flying reptile had a beak much larger than the one Rhamphorynchus had. But Pteranodon's had no teeth, even though it was a fish eater.

Pteranodon's body was as big as a chicken's and had almost no tail. Its wings spread 24 feet (7½ meters). A thick, hollow rod stuck out from the back of its head, which was as long as its body. Paleontologists now think that the rod may have been an anchor for tendons that were also attached to Pteranodon's jaws. The muscles acted as shock absorbers, to keep Pteranodon from breaking its neck, when it struck the surface of the water as it dived for fish.

All the pterosaurs had very small, weak feet. For a long time, paleontologists doubted that they could walk. Now, footprints have been discovered that show these flying reptiles could walk on all fours.

The pterosaurs had large eyes. They needed good eyesight to spot fish far below them in the water.

Pterosaurs also had large brains, which they needed to coordinate their eyesight with their sense of balance, as they soared and dove.

Some of the pterosaur fossils show fine markings that probably were hairs. This means that some of these flying reptiles, especially the later ones such as Pteranodon, were covered with fur. This probably means that they were warm-blooded animals.

Feathered Dinosaurs

At the same time that reptiles were beginning to develop wings, there were some kinds of small dinosaurs—not much bigger than a chicken—running on their hind legs and chasing insects. These little dinosaurs had

very light bones and could run swiftly and leap. By the time reptiles had begun to fly, the small dinosaurs had developed wings and feathers; they had become birds.

The first fossil of these feathered dinosaurs was discovered in a German mine in 1861. It was a very remarkable fossil because it clearly showed feathers. Dr. Karl Haberlein, a local doctor, got possession of the fossil for the money the mine owners owed him for medical services. He wanted to sell it for 700 British pounds. The German government would not pay the price. But the British Museum managed to raise the money and bought the fossil. After study, Richard Owen, named the prehistoric bird *Archaeopteryx* (ar-kee-OP-ter-iks). This name means "ancient bird."

Archaeopteryx was about the size of a pigeon. Its tail was longer than its body. Each one of the bones that made up the tail had a feather attached to it. Long feathers covered its wings, as they do in modern birds. Near the front of each wing were three free-moving fingers tipped with claws.

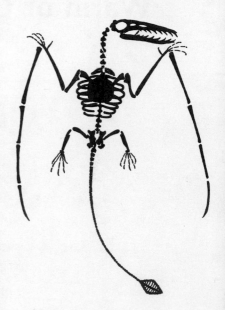

Skeletons of Rhamphorhynchus, a flying reptile, below, and a view of its arms, showing the extension of the fourth finger.

Because the wing skeleton was too small, Archaeopteryx could not fly. For a long time paleontologists thought that Archaeopteryx climbed on rocks and into the branches of trees, spread it wings, and glided to the ground. Now, many paleontologists believe, Archaeopteryx lived entirely on the ground. It chased insects, using its wings to sweep them to where it could grasp them in its beak.

Archaeopteryx was like a bird because it had birdlike hips and shoulder bones, feathers, and hollow bones. It was more like a reptile because it had teeth and did not have a horny beak. Many paleontologists consider Archaeopteryx to have been a small dinosaur with feathers. It definitely was one of the first ancestors of modern birds.

Toward the end of the Age of Reptiles, other feathered birds had followed Archaeopteryx. One of them was Hesperornis (hess-per-ORN-iss), which means "western bird," and refers to this bird's fossils being found in Kansas. Hesperornis was a swimming, diving bird, similar to the modern loon. It was 4½ feet (1⅓ meters long). It had a long sharp beak lined with teeth for catching and holding the fish it ate. It had webbed feet like modern birds that live in water, such as geese and loons. Unlike its modern descendants, Hesperornis could not walk on land because its legs were located very far back—almost at its tail. If it moved about on land at all, it probably slid along on its belly and breast, pushing with its feet, as hair seals do today. Just as some land reptiles went to live in the sea, the bird ancestors of Hesperornis did the same.

Rarely, the fossil bones of another, much smaller bird, are found near those of Hesperornis. It was Icthyornis (ik-thee-OR-niss), or "fish bird." It was about the size of a pigeon. It had large, strong wings, moved by big muscles anchored to its strong breastbone. It flew well, catching fish in its toothed beak as it swooped down to the surface of the water.

Warm or Cold Blooded?

Dinosaurs ruled the Age of Reptiles, so of course they were reptiles. But were they? Many paleontologists are saying no, and they have set off a revolution in paleontology. Actually, what they are saying is that dinosaurs were warm-blooded. Since reptiles are cold-blooded, it has always been taken for granted that dinosaurs, being reptiles, were cold-blooded, too. But if they were not, then dinosaurs should not be called true reptiles. Let us see how that argument goes.

First, there are better words than warm-blooded and cold-blooded for what we are going to talk about. The scientific word for warm-blooded is *endothermic* (en-doe-THERM-ik). It is made up of the Greek words "endo," which means "internal" or "inside," and "thermic," which means "pertaining to heat." So, endothermic means pertaining to inside heat. Endothermic animals get their body heat from processes that go on within their bodies. The bodies of mammals—such animals as dogs, lions, eagles, and whales—are endothermic. They are kept at a constant temperature, even when the air or water around them are warmer or cooler.

The scientific word for cold-blooded is *ectothermic*. "Ecto" means outside, so ectothermic means "pertaining to outside heat." The bodies of such animals as fish, frogs, worms, insects, and lizards are just about as warm or as cool as the air or water surrounding them. So, they get their body temperatures from the world outside themselves—they are ectothermic.

Saying that animals have warm or cold blood is an old fashioned way of saying that they are endothermic or ectothermic.

A lizard lying on the sand in the Arizona desert at night will become as cool as the sand and the air around it. Its body temperature will go down many degrees. The body temperatures of a fox and a cactus wren sleeping nearby will go down only a little more than one degree. At dawn, the fox and the cactus wren can immediately run and fly, but the cold lizard will barely be able to move. It will have to wait for the sun to warm it before it can run about.

At noon, if the lizard were attacked by the fox, it would have to scurry quickly to hide under a rock where the fox could not reach it. If the fox came upon the lizard far from a rock it could dart under, the lizard would surely be caught, because it could run fast for only a short distance. The fox, able to run fast for long distances, would surely overtake the lizard.

Why couldn't the lizard, a reptile, run fast for a long distance? Why could the fox, which is a mammal?

The hearts of reptiles have three divisions, or chambers. In a three-chambered heart, fresh, oxygen-laden blood from the lungs mixes with spent, carbon-dioxide laden blood from the muscles and other parts of the body.

The hearts of mammals have four chambers. They keep fresh and spent blood separate.

Animals get energy for walking, running, climbing, jumping, swimming, and flying by burning food with oxygen carried in their blood. Since reptiles' blood carries less oxygen than mammals' blood, the reptiles get less energy from their food. They cannot be as active for as long as mammals can. This is why the lizard could not run long enough to escape from the fox. Indeed, the reptiles alive today spend most of their lives lying motionless on their bellies, because they do not have enough energy to remain standing for very long. After they move quickly to catch their prey or escape from animals that prey on them, reptiles must take long rests to allow their bodies time to produce more energy.

What does this have to do with dinosaurs? If dinosaurs were true reptiles, they would have been very sluggish, not being able to run fast or fight. These activities require much energy. Walking on the hind legs, as all meat eating dinosaurs did, takes extra energy. For allosaurs to kill a brontosaur took a great amount of energy. For Triceratops to fight an attacking Tyrannosaurus also took a great deal of energy. It would be foolish to believe that all these violent activities were done in a sluggish, slow motion manner. So, many paleontologists argue, the only way dinosaurs could have gotten the energy they needed was to have the mammal type heart that pumped oxygen-fresh blood.

Today, the only animals that have four-chambered hearts are mammals, and mammals are endothermic. So, dinosaurs probably were endothermic.

You remember that the lizard in the desert had to wait for the sun to warm it before it could move about. The lizard was a small animal. In small animals, the surface of the body is large when compared to the animal's weight. The sun shining on the skin of the small lizard soon warmed up its little body.

In a big animal, the surface of its body is small when compared to its weight. The sun shining on a Tyrannosaurus cooled by the chill night air would take hours to warm it—if it were a true ectothermic reptile. And it would take a long time for warmth at the surface of Tyrannosaurus's skin to move several feet to the inside of its body. It is hard to believe that this very active meat eater would have to lie around for hours waiting for the sun to warm it enough to be able to move in search of a Triceratops to eat. It would have been even worse in the time of Allosaurus and Brachiosaurus. The Allosaurus, being much smaller than its intended prey would have warmed up first in the morning. Then it would have found a herd of brachiosaurs lying around waiting for the sun to warm them enough to get up and start eating. When they were in this condition, so many brachiosaurs could have been killed by a single allosaur that this meat eater and some of its smaller cousins would have wiped out the huge plant eaters. The same is true for the brontosaurs and diplodocuses. But this did not happen. The gigantic dinosaurs were alert enough to defend themselves and live for millions of years alongside their meat eating enemies.

This all shows that dinosaurs body temperatures did not depend on outside temperatures—they were not ectothermic.

Some dinosaur fossils have been found inside the Arctic Circle, where it never becomes really warm. Even in the Cretaceous period when this dinosaur lived, the Arctic was fairly cold and it was dark during the winter months. These are not conditions that would warm an ectotherm enough to go about the activities of its daily life. This dinosaur had to be an endotherm.

Bones not only support an animal, but they are very important in the animal's life processes. The inside of bones—the marrow—is where blood cells are manufactured. The cells then pass into the bloodstream through small blood vessels that pass through the bone. These small blood vessels go through the bone in holes, or canals, called Haversian canals. Mammals and birds have many of these canals; reptiles have very few.

A French paleontologist has recently shown that dinosaurs' bones have many Haversian canals. This means that they were like mammal and bird bones—the bones of endothermic animals. Those paleontologists who do not believe that dinosaurs were endothermic, point out that some modern reptiles have many Haversian canals, and some birds have very few.

Zoologists, the scientists who study animals—living or extinct—have divided them up into groups. One of these groupings is called a *class*. The class that dinosaurs are in is *Reptilia*, or reptiles. Dinosaurs were put into this class because their bones are like those of all reptiles. But now some paleontologists are saying, "Let us take dinosaurs out of the class of reptiles and give them a separate class called *Dinosauria*. Although dinosaurs are like reptiles in their bony structure, they were unlike them in other parts of their bodies and the way they lived." Other paleontologists answer, "We can see the dinosaurs' bones. We can't see their hearts and the ways you say they must have lived. Although you are not entirely wrong, we will keep on calling dinosaurs reptiles until you give us more proof."

The End of the Reign

At the end of the Mesozoic era, when dinosaurs had ruled animal life for 120 million years, they disappeared very suddenly. No one knows why.

Paleontologists and other scientists have thought up several reasons why these large animals died out so quickly. No one has come up with a completely convincing reason.

It would be very helpful if we knew how long it took the dinosaurs to die out. Was it a year or two, ten thousand years, or a million? (Remember that a million years is "suddenly" in the very long fossil record).

Let us examine at least two of the reasons that have been devised to explain the end of the dinosaurs.

At the end of the Mesozoic era, the climate became sharply cooler and drier all over the earth. This killed the thick, spongy marsh plants on which plant-eating dinosaurs lived. As their food plants became scarcer, the plant eaters began to die out. Soon, both lack of food and attacks by meat eaters, killed off all the plant eaters. As the plant eaters were dying out, the meat eaters were losing their source of food and were dying out, too. This is an old idea. We now know that many kinds of dinosaurs lived far from the swampy lowlands, and among the plants they ate were several kinds that did not die out—they are still living today. And the dinosaurs that ate these plants did not have to die out for lack of food.

Another reason given for the swift end of the dinosaurs was that certain small mammals, which appeared near the end of the Mesozoic era, took to eating dinosaur eggs. The mammals, being warm blooded and bearing fur, were able to increase in number as the climate became colder and their dinosaur enemies had trouble with the cold. Finally, the mammals ate enough dinosaur eggs to wipe out the big animals. The trouble with this idea is that small mammals lived alongside dinosaurs for about 100 million of the 120 million years that dinosaurs lived. During these millions of years, the small mammals were stealing dinosaurs' eggs. Also, dinosaurs probably were warm blooded and ovoviviparus. So they were not bothered by a cold climate nor by egg-stealing mammals.

The most modern guess at why dinosaurs suddenly disappeared is that a comet or a big meteor collided with the earth. It hurled into the air a vast amount of dust, which took a few years to settle to the ground. The dust prevented sunlight from reaching the earth's surface. This caused trees, bushes, grass, and other green plants to die. The plant eaters starved to death, so the meat eaters starved, too. The only animals that survived were small mammals which could live on roots and buried seeds from the dead plants.

If this idea has merit, the lack of sunlight that killed land plants, should have done the same to sea plants. Then, at the same time the dinosaurs became extinct, the sea reptiles of the Mesozoic era should have died out, too. They did. The trouble with this idea is that some fairly large animals—crocodiles, giant sea-turtles, for example—did survive the time when dinosaurs all died out. Also, scientists are having trouble proving that a comet or meteor collided with the earth just at the time dinosaurs died out.

Still other ideas are a world wide epidemic of a disease that killed only dinosaurs. But, at the time of the dinosaurs, the spread of disease all over the world was just about impossible. It might be that the explosion of a nearby star, sent to earth so much deadly radiation that it killed the dinosaurs. This idea does not explain why other animals were not killed by the radiation.

So, you can see that none of these ideas are really satisfactory. Can you think up a new one?